FRANK LLOYD WRIGHT'S
HOUSES

Thomas A. Heinz

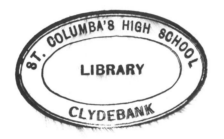

Frank Lloyd Wright's
HOUSES

Thomas A. Heinz

GRANGE BOOKS

This 2002 edition is published by Grange Books An imprint of Grange Books plc Units 1 - 6 Kingsnorth Industrial Estate Hoo, Nr. Rochester, Kent, ME3 9ND

www.grangebooks.co.uk

Printed in Italy

ISBN 1 84013 470 4

Dedicated to Don & Virginia Lovness, possibly Frank Lloyd Wright's most sensitive clients, for whom he designed two houses.

It is essential that a workable system of preservation and restoration be co-ordinated between the existing owners of the many remaining examples of Frank Lloyd Wright's buildings for, unless they are maintained in their original colours, materials and arrangements, how can anyone make a proper assessment of their worth, even to the point of whether they like them or not. An assessment cannot be made based on photographs, or on memories of buildings that no longer reflect the work as Wright conceived, approved and personally directed its execution. Wright's work is too important to allow further deterioration and demolition and readers must try to participate in this effort of preservation, even if it is only to involve others in an appreciation of Wright's work.

Why did Frank Lloyd Wright design so many houses? His response to this question was 'because people ask me to!' Wright was willing to design anything: houses, offices, churches and synagogues, gas stations, garages, chairs and tables, stained glass, silver tea services, magazine covers, dinnerware, table cloths, dog and cat houses, colleges, and even dresses for his clients' wives.

Wright understood the strong emotions surrounding a house as home, the place connected with one's most intimate life. He would show the client a drawing, suggest an idea, an outlook, a point of view with relation to nature with a capital 'N'. This was a revelation to them and one that they could not easily experience elsewhere.

Harriet Freeman was a case in point: the Freeman House in Los Angeles was built in 1924, and she

FRANK LLOYD WRIGHT HOUSE AND STUDIO, OAK PARK, ILLINOIS, 1889–1909

The first mature design by Wright was a very sophisticated one for himself in which his sense of proportion and love of complex geometry is at once apparent. It is less fussy than the contemporaneous buildings of Joseph L. Silsbee, and much simpler than those of his subsequent employer and mentor, Louis Sullivan.

Wright worked on his house over a period of nearly ten years, adding a studio in 1895. It shows admirably how Wright's aesthetic was developing over the years.

FRANK LLOYD WRIGHT HOUSE, OAK PARK, ILLINOIS, 1889 (SOUTH-WEST EXTERIOR)

lived in her Wright design into the 1980s, finding that the house was revealing something new to her every day, a fact which continued to delight her throughout the 60 years she had lived there.

Wright was not a good businessman himself, nor was he an astute economist. He realized, however, that building homes was a more manageable proposition

and, because of their size, less likely to be problematical and rather more interesting. Moreover, there was greater demand for houses than for public buildings and Wright was more disposed to specialize in them at this time. Residential projects present more variables; while sites for office buildings are normally flat and square and mass housing is best built on a flat, open parcel of land, the terrain can vary considerably in the case of houses designed for individual clients. The site of the

Heurtley House of Oak Park is probably the flattest, and is a nearly square site, but customized, individual designs can be built anywhere, the more site obstacles the better, as these are the factors that bring character to a design: imagine how the Millard House of Pasadena or Fallingwater would have looked on a flat plot! However, the client requirements for an office building may be more straightforward than a residential design, especially at the upper end of the housing market where an individual can afford to indulge himself.

Why is house design so important? Because people live, love and raise their families in them and there is nothing more potent than the concept of home. Not everyone works in an office but, whatever their job, everyone goes home.

Wright's houses were a departure from the traditional; not everyone liked them when they first appeared, and some do not like them to this day. In Wright's lifetime, there were fewer than 1,000 different designs, many of them for repeat clients, though only a few took the opportunity to work one-to-one with Wright and experience his dynamic approach first-hand.

There are more design options in houses than in offices: while there may be a special feature in a public lobby or the boss's office, the rest of the space is likely to be more prosaic. In houses, there exist a variety of function in the form of living and dining rooms, bedrooms,

CHARNLEY HOUSE, CHICAGO, ILLINOIS, 1891

This house originated from Adler & Sullivan's architectural practice, though the actual designer is not known for sure. Adler and Sullivan, though dedicated to their profession, were out to make money, with the result that residential designs were not a priority and were left to the junior staff. This suggests that Wright may have had a hand in the design, the result of which is an avant-garde building of great restraint, which might just as well have been a spaceship, so extraordinary was it for its time.

The design builds on Sullivan's initial ideas and simplifies them, as Wright would continue to do in his own work later on.

family rooms and the many other ways of utilizing space for a multitude of applications.

At first, Wright's attention was focused on his own locality, where he produced designs for friends and neighbours. As time passed and he became more successful, his circle of influence widened and by 1900 examples of his work were well distributed throughout metro-

GEORGE BLOSSOM HOUSE, CHICAGO, ILLINOIS, 1892

Although Wright was trained in design and building by Cecil Corwin while working in Silsbee's Chicago office, and to a lesser degree at Adler & Sullivan's, the Blossom house meets and possibly exceeds anything produced by his mentors, even at this early date. Wright's understanding of materials and proportions are clearly in evidence in the shiplapping and closely spaced balusters above the entry porch. The brick base, visible through the mass of planting around the foundation outline, is constructed using a refined iron-spot Roman brick, which Wright would use again on the Winslow house just a few years later.

Chicago; ten years later, his buildings could be found from California to New York, and by the end of his life in North and Central America, Europe as well as Asia – only in Africa and Australia were there no examples of his work.

Were there regional influences or differences? These were not as great as one might imagine. The same 'desert masonry', developed at Ocotillo and Taliesin West, was used not only in the Arizona desert, but also in the cooler regions of the upper Hudson Valley of New York. There were wooden-clad houses in the far north as well as in California's Santa Barbara area, and brick was used from Minnesota to Alabama, while there was as much care with the flashing of a roof in wet regions as there was in a dry. Roofs with deep overhangs occurred in the north as well as the south.

While some of Wright's buildings appeared to possess ethnic qualities, such as the 'Mayan'-looking California concrete block houses, this was not Wright's actual intention. The climate of Chicago's south side, though not very different from certain parts of Japan, was not the reason for the Japanese appearance of the Foster House; it seemed that Wright liked the style and used it well. Wright's work was not totally without outside influences, however, and these were injected into his designs in ways quite different from their origins.

It is not important to identify precisely the source of Wright's inspiration, since in any case this is open to speculation. Wright himself only admitted to a few influences, mostly literary, at the end of the 1943 edition of his autobiography, and included Laotzu, Buddha, Jesus, Walt Whitman, Henry Thoreau, and his mentor, Louis Sullivan. He also mentioned Gene Masselink, the only one of his apprentices referred to by name.

Some architects are not even aware of their sources of inspiration, having absorbed ideas as a gradual process over time. There was a period, just as Wright was beginning, when it was the practice to consult 'pattern books' when designing a building. These contained measured drawings of mostly historical buildings, and would include not only full façades, but also architectural details which could be traced off and incorporated into a finished design. This method gave some idea of proportion in

WALTER GALE HOUSE, OAK PARK, ILLINOIS, 1893

A series of modest houses in much the same style followed on the heels of Wright's own house, two of which were built on a speculative basis for Wright's neighbour, Walter Gale, while others were for Robert

Emmond and Francis Woolly. There were small differences in roof profiles but, apart from that, the plans were nearly all identical. The houses appear to be small but are in fact quite roomy, while the walls of the bays consist mainly of windows.

terms of the overall scheme, as well as the individual parts, which not only hastened the design process, but was also an excellent teaching aid for draftsmen.

One needs to examine what Wright actually achieved, when one will see what, in his case, has been called 'evidence of intelligence'. We can perceive the conscious experiments he was conducting, and which for the most part were accomplished with his clients' approval, as can be seen from correspondence between them. As with all experiments which test design to the limits, some succeeded, while others did not.

Most of Wright's houses could be considered purpose-built. Some included elements in addition to the purely domestic, such as stables and garages, guest suites, water services and others. This was a natural progression from Wright's early life when he had worked on his uncles' farms. Besides farmhouses, these not only have barns, tool and storage sheds, but also garages for cars and stables for horses.

This application can be seen in Wright's first project, the Winslow house and its stable, which was home to horses, automobiles and the printing press that Winslow used for his Auvergne Press publishing company. On it was produced, not only the famous *House Beautiful*, a book written by a close friend of Wright's uncle Jenkin Lloyd Jones, William Gannett, but also the lesser known but more impressive, *Eve of St. Agnes*, printed with the assistance of Winslow's friend and neighbour, Chauncey Williams, himself an important publisher and a Wright client.

Other purpose building was a small laboratory designed for Peter Beachy at the end of his garage opposite the chauffeur's quarters.

However, most of the houses had all the services contained within the main structure: Herbert Johnson's house, Wingspread, had the garages incorporated in a service wing, as did the John Gillin House.

These multi-functional designs also include the Dana House, its studio accessed through a long two-storey passageway; Wright's own Oak Park house and studio; the Darwin D. Martin House, with its garage and conservatory; Taliesin, home of the Fellowship; the Allen House surrounding a pool; Aline Barnsdall's Hollyhock House, Isabelle Martin's Greycliff, the Hanna House, Fallingwater and the Lowell Walter House and boathouse.

Wright's buildings evolved in a way that mirrored society and the changes that were occurring. In the earliest years of his career, he had followed the status quo to a certain degree and had included facilities for such Victorian conventions as receiving guests and keeping servants, as well as providing formal dining rooms and stables.

Houses were usually in neighbourhoods, had front façades that were carefully contrived and rear ones that were less so. They were highly decorated in the over-exuberant style of the day, with art-glass windows and finely turned and carved furniture. For the most part, the major rooms – living rooms, dining rooms and entrance halls – were on the first floor, with bedrooms on the second.

As the years passed, so the Victorian way of life eroded. First to go were the servants, leaving their masters to fend for themselves and streamline their lives, which heralded the Art Deco style. Modern conveniences began to make an appearance, such as clothes washing machines and vacuum cleaners. As cars became more in evidence, the garages remained, but not the chauffeurs. Stained glass went out of fashion and was replaced by windows with panes divided by thin wooden or metal muntins.

As life styles became more individualized and unconventional, so did Wright's choice of materials: who would have predicted the wonderful effect of square, grey concrete blocks in the California concrete block houses of the 1920s?

Then the Second World War effected more changes, with economy of production on everyone's mind; extraneous details were eliminated if deemed unnecessary. Gone were all forms of decoration and attempts at beautification; it was back to bare essentials in a period of austerity which lasted until well after the end of the war, when the housing boom exploded and more land was made available for housing. Building lots became larger and the ratio between land and construction costs became much lower. Garages were eliminated in favour of what are now termed carports.

When one thinks of Frank Lloyd Wright, one pictures the long, horizontal lines of the Prairie houses, satisfying because of Wright's understanding of people and the elements important for successful human habitation.

Wright changed structural and visual engineering, making certain elements, such as posts and walls, more substantial, and seemingly more capable of supporting the heavy loads placed upon them; this was in contrast to the spindly structures which supported many a Californian house, and which clung precariously to the sides of steep hillsides.

The traditional view of Wright's career is that it can be divided into four phases: his early life, the Prairie era, the years when his personal life was in disarray, and the Usonian era. Each of these periods produced designs with certain characteristics in common, which is not to say that all the houses in the chronology looked the same. Moreover, there are certain points where Wright is clearly following new directions in

WILLIAM H. WINSLOW HOUSE, RIVER FOREST, ILLINOIS, 1893

This was Wright's first independent commission after leaving Adler & Sullivan's and is a bold statement of his thinking at the time. It is a work that has been much imitated without being thoroughly understood. Most striking is the heavy roof form with overhanging eaves that throws the top storey into shadow and accentuates the simple, symmetrical lower façade with its fine Roman brickwork. It also brings into dramatic relief the sparkling crispness of the doorway, with its squarish front door, and of the window surrounds, and contrasts well with the assymetrical rear elevation.

ROBERT W. ROLOSON ROW HOUSES, CHICAGO, ILLINOIS, 1894
During the design of these town houses it is possible that Wright began to develop an appreciation of suburban and rural situations.

Although these houses appear typical of other brownstones, they have a distinctive quality of their own; the brickwork is superb and the groupings of the mullioned windows have a Gothic flavour

clearly not intended by Wright. There were once beautiful terracotta railings and balusters surrounding each of the small front gardens, which were sadly removed many years ago.

WILLIAM H. WINSLOW STABLES, RIVER FOREST, ILLINOIS, 1897

The Winslow house of 1893 was possibly Wright's most important independent commission. He was to design many outbuildings for his houses, but this is the first and is still one of the best. The stables, erected several years after the main house was built, were designed to accommodate carriages as well as horses and there were several other rooms intended for other activities, which included space for Winslow's printing press. The second level consisted of the servants' quarters.

his work. Moreover, wthin each of these phases there are many anomalies.

THE EARLY YEARS 1886–1900
Wright was referred to as a 'boy architect' when he was indeed little more than a boy. His uncle, the Rev. Jenkin Lloyd Jones had hired a former Syracuse architect, Joseph Lyman Silsbee, recently arrived in Chicago, to design a small chapel for the family in the Jones Valley, Wisconsin, and Wright is said to have assisted in the project. Silsbee tended to specialize in houses rather than churches but had previously

been commissioned to design a residential-type building for the Rev. Jones' Chicago parish of All Souls, on the near south side of Chicago.

Wright had visited Chicago and All Souls during its construction, where he had became acquainted with Silsbee, who eventually employed him: Jones managed to secure lodgings for his nephew with the family of a draftsman who also worked for Silsbee's company.

Silsbee was working on some family houses in the Chicago area when Wright went to work for him. There were several houses for a client called Waller, who does not

B. HARLEY BRADLEY HOUSE, KANKAKEE, ILLINOIS, 1900

This house heralded the beginning of the first great period of Wright's career. It is a model of simplicity with stucco walls, the windows organized, gathered and tied together by bands of wood trim. Wright removed all ornament from trim and surfaces, leaving it confined to the windows that were characterized by a severe geometry. It is wonderfully situated on the north shore of the Kankakee river, so one wonders why it was not oriented towards it rather than the street.

18

WARD W. WILLITTS HOUSE, HIGHLAND PARK, ILLINOIS, 1901

This has been described as 'the first masterpiece among the Prairie houses', and there is no doubt that it is one of the finest of its genre. Wright based the house on a Greek Cross, the rooms connecting at the centre. The long, low hipped roof extends from the porte-cochère at the right, penetrates the two-storey central wing and connects with the porch at the end. This was the start of other cross-based houses, though each have variations according to their site.

appear to be related to Edward C. Waller, Wright's future client. These and many others for the same client, were later built in Edgewater.

The head of Silsbee's drafting room was a young man called Cecil Corwin, and it was Corwin who was to educate Wright in the

complexities of the architectural profession and life in general. Corwin and Wright hit it off immediately and became close friends, spending as much time together out of the office as they did inside it. However, Wright was ambitious and soon progressed to the architectural practice of Adler & Sullivan, once he felt himself to be proficient.

Adler & Sullivan's was considered to be the most advanced design practice in Chicago. Wright was taken on by Sullivan himself to assist him in the design for the revolutionary Auditorium Building, the tower of which would be the future home of Adler & Sullivan's, with adjacent offices for Sullivan and Wright overlooking Lake Michigan. The

pratice continued to design commercial buildings, leaving the bread-and-butter residential designs to the young Wright.

Wright had met a young girl at his uncle's church and decided to marry her. Needing a home, he borrowed $5,000 from Sullivan to enable him to build a house. Wright had already been living for a time in Oak Park in the home of an

FB Henderson House, Elmhurst, Illinois, 1901

The full scope of Wright's genius at this time is expressed in his plastered wooden houses, of which this is a mature example. It was a development of the Hickox house built about a year earlier and is in some ways identical to it.

30 in Oak Park and the neighbouring suburb of River Forest.

Most of these houses are typical of this early period, being of a more traditional design. They are well-proportioned with interesting elements such as patterned shingles, turrets, rounded porches, and decorated gables. By and large, houses by other designers had adhered to the English tradition, and while Wright's work also contained certain historicist elements, there was always something different or unusual in the details or proportions.

Wright's houses were more geometrical but not always simpler. The interiors nearly always had larger rooms and there were fireplaces set in the living rooms, marking the centre of the house. Not all of them had porches and of

associate of the Rev. Jones, a Unitarian pastor. Wright bought himself a plot on a deep corner site, and designed his house in the tradition he had learned from Silsbee, but in a rather more simplified form. The house was added to after his family had increased from four to six children.

Then Wright decided to go it alone, and brought his own

practice to the house he had designed just three years after leaving the Adler & Sullivan offices.

Wright was a sociable and gregarious person and entertained a great deal, with the result that neighbours soon began to want their own Wright house. There were eventually 14 of his designs within several blocks of his own house, which was to grow to over

William G. Fricke House, Oak Park, Illinois, 1902

This is one of the tallest of the Oak Park houses and appears to be a case of Wright experimenting with the vertical, rather than a continuation of the more established, essentially horizontal style. However, it retains all the other characteristics of the Prairie style. Constructed on three floors, the elements are placed with a certain randomness, giving a feeling of a group of various parts rather than a unified whole; the effect is rather emphasized by the dark outlining of the horizontals.

those that did, not all of them were roofed over. The sense of rhythm that Silsbee injected into his houses does not appear in Wrights' until the Prairie era, when it is expressed in the three horizontal bands of which the houses were composed. The base or first band of a Silsbee house was brick or more commonly, stone, which may have been flagstone or random ashlar, and the brick was more often red. The next band consisted of the walls, offset by an upper and lower line of trim, usually an ogee moulding. The upper and third band constituted the second and, on occasion, the third floors. It included gables and more often gambrel roofs, dormers, and groupings of arched windows.

The Prairie Era 1900–1910

This period produced Wright's most popular and famous designs which, had they been his only output, would still have made him one of the masters of architecture. The

ARTHUR HEURTLEY HOUSE, OAK PARK, ILLINOIS, 1902

Arthur Heurtley was a banker at the prestigious Northern Trust Company in Chicago and his house certainly gives an impression of wealth and security, the canted walls adding to its feeling of solidity. The brick prow that defines the porch clearly indicates the front entrance, but is not an overt invitation to enter. This is a fine example of Wright's early Prairie style; the long, low horizontal and dark Roman brick seems to recall a single-storey log cabin, the horizontal emphasized by the protruding brick courses and the continuous frieze of windows.

Prairie style is a descendant of the Shingle style of Henry Hobson Richardson which was adopted by Silsbee. The name suggests the wide open spaces of the Wild West, a world of log cabins with overhanging eaves, low-pitched roofs, single storeys and simple interiors. At this time, Wright was developing his own unified system of building, a style that others were never fully able to emulate, not even his colleagues at this time.

The buildings present a simplified appearance, integrated into the site by means of emphatic horizontal planes. Rooms as boxes are replaced by open spaces,

loosely divided by screens or panels. Decoration is kept to the minimum, except where the materials dictate. Main rooms are often above ground level to give better all-round views and light-screen windows replace rectangular window holes in walls, which are of plain stucco and brick. All services (plumbing, etc) are incorporated into the building as architectural features, while furnishings are designed to be in accord with the building. Moreover, no 'fashionable' decorators were to be employed.

These Prairie buildings continued what Silsbee had begun,

GEORGE BARTON HOUSE, BUFFALO, NEW YORK, 1903

This was the first of Wright's Buffalo projects, the thread linking them all together being the Larkin company. The Barton House is a near-duplicate of the J.J. Walser House, built for a relative of one of Darwin Martin's associates at the Larkin company on Chicago's far west side. The difference is that it was surfaced with stucco. Martin wanted an economical building to test Wright's ability to design houses before he chose the plan for his own brother-in-law, George Barton. Included in the interior are some built-in pieces that are among Wright's best work.

the three-part rhythm of the exterior scheme. Wright kept the low concrete base, though greatly reduced it over the Silsbee solution, while the walls again were simplified from the Silsbee examples. Wright's roofs were mostly hipped and were given less steep slopes for the climatic conditions of the upper Midwest. Roof slopes became more pronounced where there were harsher winters, being better able to cast off snow. Low, sloping roofs, however, are more susceptible to leakages, a perennial problem for Wright, but which was possibly due to lack of maintenance

rather than a fault in design.

The words 'always' and 'never' cannot be used with confidence where Wright's work is concerned. It is said that there is always an exception to every rule, and Wright introduced many exceptions into his work in an attempt to 'mix things up', as he would remark from time to time.

When Wright was still a child, his mother, Anna, had discovered a kindergarten system, developed by Friedrich Froebel, in which it was believed that play materials and practical occupations were needed to develop a child's real nature and help them to develop creative

FRANCIS W. LITTLE HOUSE, PEORIA, ILLINOIS, 1903

The plan of this first house for Francis Little is similar to that of the Dana House, as is the arched front door, and the interior was as elaborate in many respects although the art glass was uninspired, leading one to think that Wright was concentrating all his efforts on the Dana House, which also had its conception around this time.

Another Peoria client, Robert Clarke, later bought the house for which Wright designed some additions and alterations.

Little had liked his Peoria house so much that about ten years later he had Wright design another, larger house for him in Wayzata.

27

EDWIN CHENEY HOUSE, OAK PARK, ILLINOIS, 1904

The one-storey house seems dwarfed by the large, mature trees which surround it. It is sited on a ridge that runs north–south through Oak Park and beyond, with the wing walls to each side of the front porch set on *the edge of the ridge. At the rear of the house, the yard drops away and exposes a basement wall, originally intended to be an interior garage. The large, gently sloping roof surmounts large wooden trusses that hold it and the ceilings below it in place. In the back of the central* *fireplace is a window that directs light down through a brick shaft within the chimney and into the back hallway. The light is diffused by a wonderful art-glass window.*

Wright and Cheney's wife, Mamah, later had an affair with tragic consequences.

28

**SUSAN LAWRENCE DANA HOUSE,
SPRINGFIELD, ILLINOIS, 1903** (RIGHT
AND BELOW)

*This is a large house set on a
relatively small urban site and
encompasses the original house that
Susan's father had purchased years
earlier. This was a Victorian design,
so certain compromises had to be
made in the design and it is not
typical of a Prairie house.*

*It contains some of the finest
examples of Wright's genius in
several categories. The art glass is
unsurpassed in both design and
execution, and there are some
unique items of furniture, one of
which combines wood and art glass
in a freestanding piece, together with
the famous print table and pieces of
sculpture integrated into the interior.*

*The Dana house was published
in the Wasmuth portfolios, a
collection of Wright's drawings
published in Berlin in 1910.*

DARWIN D. MARTIN HOUSE,
BUFFALO, NEW YORK, 1904 (THIS
PAGE AND OPPOSITE)

*This is a masterpiece of the
horizontal form with few verticals,
the hipped roof adding to a feeling
of tranquillity. The proportions of
the building in relation to the site
are ideal, but it is unfortunate that
so much of the original
construction was demolished in the
1950s, when the garage,
conservatory and greenhouses
were lost. Recently, the apartment
buildings that were built in their
place were demolished to make
way for the rebuilding of these lost
elements. The interior is one of the
most complex of the Prairie era.*

ideas. Wright seems to have benefited from his education, and this is reflected in his later career; his gift for abstraction is most evident in his art glass, which he introduced to windows and lightscreens, and which is characterized by geometric borders and segments composed of glass and metal. While other designers of the period favoured translucent, coloured glass, Wright liked to use clear glass in windows that were not only decorative, but which allowed the outside world into the house, sometimes incorporating flora and fauna in highly stylized forms. Colours were restricted to mostly earth tones.

With the turn of the new century, Wright had found a new freedom, perhaps inspired by the emerging social order that was challenging Victorian values on all levels. Houses had previously been formal, requiring rooms for specific purposes; Wright was no longer seeing rooms as boxes but as spaces which could flow one into another, creating a feeling of even greater space and defining a new way of living. This sense of visual space and distance added considerable excitement to his interiors and gave Wright many more options for the arrangement of furniture and lighting.

Although there are no old-style parlours in Wright buildings of this time, there were occasional reception rooms, some of which were reduced to a bench or a quiet niche by an entry door, while others were actual rooms with doors or heavy curtains separating them from other parts of the house.

These Prairie buildings were constructed using traditional methods of building which included concrete foundations and brick walls with wooden laths holding interior plaster in place. While there were still attics, Wright eliminated basements in their traditional forms.

At this time, some amazing engineering innovations were emerging, which mostly went

A.P. JOHNSON HOUSE, DELAVAN LAKE, WISCONSIN, 1905

In the design of this house, the dramatic possibilities of a steep site above water have been explored to the full. It fulfils all the requirements of the perfect Prairie house, with its long, low-pitched overhanging roofs, ribbon windows, massive piers, and extensions onto the garden. However, the building has since been resurfaced and the interior remodelled to such an extent that it is now barely recognizable as a Wright design.

unnoticed or ignored, but which resulted in the unique look that is a feature of Wright buildings.

Unlike the houses of his first period where the building itself was the main consideration, Wright began to conceive and execute complete interiors during the Prairie era, which included furniture designs, carpets, linens and other accessories, all uniquely his own.

Wright's clients were much attracted to this new total approach, which they could see for themselves in the houses Wright had designed for their friends and neighbours.

However, although Wright had aficionados, there was no actual 'following' – that would come much later in his long career.

THE LOST YEARS 1910–1932
The transition from the era of the Prairie houses to this more chaotic period was the result of Wright's decision to change his life, when he closed his successful Oak Park studio, transferring his practice to remote and rural Wisconsin. He left his wife and family and began to cohabit with the wife of a former client after two years spent in

WILLIAM A. GLASNER HOUSE, GLENCOE, ILLINOIS, 1905

Built along the upper edge of a ravine which feeds water into Lake Michigan, the house assumes a horizontal floor line, the base following the ups and downs of the ravine edge. Two of the rooms are octagonal, similar to the library in Wright's own studio from the 1890s, while the living room has a pitched ceiling with heavy wood-trim boards. The windows are three-part units with a large, nearly square area of plate glass in the centre, flanked by two beautiful, simplified Tree-of-Life motifs in soft iridescent colours.

Europe. This inevitably affected his clientele, though some remained faithful, but it was also a new beginning.

As Wright's life became more complicated, so did his buildings. They became more decorated than the simple Prairie houses, with embellishments here and there and, in some cases, over entire surfaces. Moreover, the spaces within these buildings were becoming more complex, with nooks and crannies, niches and soffits, when in the previous ten years, rooms could be defined by a simple balustrade.

At this time, Wright was seeking unusual solutions to what, today, is termed mass housing, and he was conceiving and executing many entirely new systems of building.

The first was the American Readi-Cut System devised for the Richards Brothers of Milwaukee, which allowed a wide variety of building types yet, within certain limits, were all of stucco trimmed with wood. The actual construction used the common and traditional stud system of assembly.

A second system was tried about ten years later, resulting in a group of buildings that became known as the California block houses. Four of these were built in Los Angeles and Pasadena, all made of 16-inch (41-cm) square concrete blocks placed on the inside and outside of an interior air space, and which included a variety of specialty blocks to accommodate corners, ventilation and windows.

THOMAS P. HARDY HOUSE, RACINE, WISCONSIN, 1905

The design of this house takes its site very much into consideration, and is all the better for it. From the street side it appears to be another compact Prairie house, complete with hipped roof and gathered windows. On the side facing Lake Michigan, however, it appears quite vertical; the interior is the first instance in which Wright has expressed a two-storey space on the exterior.

The house is symmetrical and because it is located next to a park is often mistaken for a public facility. It has a doorway at either end and one could easily assume that one was for men and the other for women.

STEPHEN M.B. HUNT HOUSE, LAGRANGE, ILLINOIS, 1907

A Wright design for a fireproof house for $5,000 was published in the April 1907 edition of the Ladies' Home Journal *and was realized in this first house for Stephen Hunt. There is a departure, however, from the published design in that it is constructed on a wooden frame with a stucco surface. The solid corners contract with the centre of each elevation that is filled with windows.*

Of note are the tall, thin borders at either end of the main group. These frame and introduce the

four-window group and without this important detail the windows would merely be four holes in a wall. The wooden trim on the exterior adds interest to the design but acts as a divider for the large areas of stucco which stabilize it and make it less subject to cracking.

Hunt later decided to move to Oshkosh, Wisconsin, and around 1917 commissioned Wright to design a second house for him. This was recently identified as one of the American Readi-Cut System bungalows though Hunt never lived in the property and it was apparently rented out.

Some buildings had over 30 variations on a theme. The blocks were several inches thick with a groove along each of the four edges. These grooves were filled with mortar and held in place with steel rods that held the entire assembly in place.

Neither of these systems worked as well as was anticipated: as with any venture, it all comes back to economics. The American System houses were perhaps too modern-looking to be widely acceptable, and the block system turned out to be much too costly to implement.

PETER A. BEACHY HOUSE, OAK PARK, ILLINOIS, 1906

The design incorporates an earlier house to the point of obliterating it on the exterior, while the original Victorian Fargo house can only be seen in a few places in the basement. It was built on the largest residential site in Oak Park and was given seven gables, though there is no evidence that there was any attempt to relate it to the popular Hawthorne story, The House of Seven Gables.

Two years earlier, Wright had done something similar with the Dana House, but Peter Beachy and his wife had simple tastes and were not overly fond of the art glass that had made Wright so famous.

A hard-burned, red brick has been utilized that has some dark areas on its face and is uneven; some bricks are warped. This type of brick was also used in several houses designed by Greene & Greene in Pasadena, California, where it is referred to as clinker brick and is generally fired much closer to the heat source than the remainder of the bricks in the kiln.

The Beachy house is set just the width of a driveway from the north lot line and aligns itself with the fronts of most of the other houses on the street so that one hardly notices the large grounds behind it.

Usonian Era 1932–1959

The important event that ushered this defining period was the formation of the Taliesin Fellowship in 1932. The Wrights had put a lot of thought and preparation into their new system for training young architects. Wright was determined that this would bring a new focus to his life and hoped to clarify his latest ideas by working through all the possible solutions. While no actual buildings came directly out

of the work of the apprentices, it is reasonable to assume that many new ideas were exchanged from which Wright would later benefit. However, Wright's most famous building came into being as a result of the school. Edgar Kaufmann, Jr. was one of the early visitors to the Fellowship, and it was through his enthusiasm for Wright and influence on his father that Fallingwater came into existence.

Wright conceived the so-called

Usonia (United States of North America) houses as low-cost homes that would be widely built throughout the community.

The construction techniques were revolutionary: traditional foundations were eliminated in favour of a ballast system, where a trench was dug and filled with coarse gravel for drainage with a small grade beam formed above it. This may have been attached to the concrete floor slab that had a grid

ISABEL ROBERTS HOUSE, RIVER FOREST, ILLINOIS, 1908

The unusual feature of this house is the extension of the ground-floor living room into the upper floor. Wright had already included the idea in his Ladies' Home Journal *project and had realized it in the Dana House, but it was the first time it had been included in a smaller design.*

The Roberts House was resurfaced with brick over the original stucco many years after its initial construction and Wright was called in by later owners to remodel the interior, when he introduced lapped boards to the ceilings, mahogany built-in cabinets in the dining room, and a balcony.

Contrary to popular belief, Isabel Roberts was not related to Charles E. Roberts or to either of Wright's clients from Kankakee, the Hickox and Bradley families. She was an architect in her own right and her talent and position in Wright's Oak Park office has been largely ignored or underestimated.

of the building etched upon it.

A new approach was brought to walls, where a plywood core of ³/₄-inch (2-cm) material was set between an inner and outer layer of solid cypress or redwood boards screwed to it. This was to add a small measure of support to the roof as well as providing insulation in cold weather. The wood had no finish applied to it and became the final wall surface inside and out.

The roofs were simplified again: this time they were mostly flat and finished in the same manner as the walls, with wood.

In the earliest days, around 1895, a central heating plant had been used, along with several radiators, usually one to each room. There was no air-conditioning. Wright adopted a new approach, laying the heating pipes below the concrete floor, which proved to be an excellent method whereby heat was transferred to the space above.

A warm floor was always a desirable feature and Wright provided it: with warm feet, the air temperature could be considerably reduced to as low as 60 degrees and still feel comfortable. There was still no air-conditioning system, but radiators were eliminated, freeing the precious floor space they had once occupied.

Wright was well aware of the need for good ventilation. He clearly understood that heat rises

FREDERICK C. ROBIE HOUSE, CHICAGO, ILLINOIS, 1909

The Robie House is perhaps one of the most sophisticated of Wright's designs still retaining characteristics of the Prairie houses. Its controlled, long, straight lines, contrasted with the rhythm of the windows, shows how far Wright had come in refining his detailing over the previous ten years. Moreover, there are several unusual engineering features present in the design.

and cold falls and added operable clerestory windows that allowed the hot air to escape and draw in the colder air below. Wright also used full banks of doors that could be opened in major rooms. These were often situated opposite the clerestories and made for a positive air flow.

Wright also began a radical simplification of the way space could be used in a house. He managed to convince clients of the savings that could be had by using the same space for many activities. Accordingly, the boundaries between living and dining rooms were reduced or eliminated.

Wright did design custom furniture for some of these Usonian houses, largely made from plywood, some of which was common fir, which in some cases was oak-veneered for a more sophisticated, finished appearance. There were so many Usonian houses that many of the same designs were used several times over, but no client seemed to mind.

The clients of this period tended to have more modest budgets than at earlier times. In 1904, Wright had published the plans of a three- to four-bedroom house with about 2,000sq ft (180m²), intended to be made of concrete. In 1936 and again in 1939 Wright built completely different houses for $5,000 for Jacobs and Pope; this was Wright's way of using new and money-saving ideas to accommodate the budgets of the clients, both of whom were newspaper journalists who later put their experiences of living in a Wright house into print. These articles attracted many clients who may never have considered using Wright's services, and turned him into a celebrity which brought in even more clients.

Wright also developed innovative systems of building throughout these years, of which there were two basic types, the first called 'Usonian Automatic', which was another concrete block system similar in some respects to the Californian example, but which involved the client in the process of building. The client produced the blocks himself and proved that he was able to build a house with his own hands. This was a good idea from the client's point of view as it gave him an economical building in which he had not only invested his money, but also the sweat of his brow.

The second was a system of prefabrication. Marshal Erdman, an architecture graduate of the University of Illinois-Urbana, had

FREDERICK C. ROBIE HOUSE, CHICAGO, ILLINOIS, 1909

The south façade of the Robie House has an exaggerated horizontal line when viewed straight-on, as this photograph shows. However, it is not usually viewed from this perspective but from the sides where the proportions seem more pleasing and larger roof cantilevers are in evidence. It is a three-story house that appears even taller. This view illustrates the three-dimensional quality of the façade.

The house was fitted out with a full range of interior appointments, most of which have long since gone. A wonderful cantilevered couch was designed for the living room that went with small tabourets for taking tea, which were used before what we now call coffee tables were developed. Custom-made rugs were produced in which the pattern between living and dining rooms was varied but which kept the same overall theme throughout.

been the contractor for Wright's Unitarian Meeting House in Madison, Wisconsin and had also produced a series of prefabricated medical buildings. He asked Wright to design some houses that he could market and several of them were built. There is more consistency in these designs than in the others Wright had attempted to this date.

CONCLUSION

Most of the architecturally important buildings throughout

history have not been houses, but Wright changed all this and produced several masterpieces into the bargain. Wright's work brought houses into focus and his influence continues to this day. Never before had so much attention been placed on the house, its design, maintenance and furnishings, all dedicated to the comfort of the occupants. While many architects have attempted to imitate what Wright achieved, Wright himself regarded this as misguided, remarking that what they needed to do instead was to concentrate on

LAURA GALE HOUSE, OAK PARK, ILLINOIS, 1909

Unlike most of the Prairie houses, Laura Gale's did not have a pitched roof with wide overhangs, but a flat one with minimal overhang. Moreover, most Prairie houses have broad sets of casement windows set below deep roof overhangs; the roofs have low pitches, usually hipped. These Prairie houses set a horizontal line marked by the trim and brick joints. However, the Laura Gale House does not quite follow this pattern. It is an extremely small house on one of the

smallest residential sites in Oak Park, set adjacent to the Beachy House which is on one of the largest. The winglets at each side of the first-floor living room were equipped with radiators that were intended to be sufficient but needed to be supplemented.

Some have compared the house to Fallingwater, but there are few similarities other than the flat roof and cantilevers.

Laura Gale was the widow of Thomas Gale, a Wright client of the 1890s, whose house is just around the corner, near Wright's studio.

TALIESIN, SPRING GREEN, WISCONSIN, 1911 (THIS PAGE AND OVERLEAF)
Taliesin was conceived as a refuge from the chaos of city life and all that had happened in Wright's turbulent personal life.

It sits on the brow of a low hill, just above the lake that feeds into the nearby Wisconsin river. Wright loved the soft yellow stone outcroppings which were a feature of the area and designed his new house to appear as one with the landscape. This, and the view overleaf, confirms that he was successful in his attempt.

It is said that the steel used in the long cantilever was from the steel bridge which once spanned the river nearby. This is called the birdwalk, as a visit there makes one feel up in the trees and at one with the birds.

Taliesin was to house Wright's immediate family as well as his office and apprentices. Sadly it was the scene of a tragedy when Mamah Cheney and her children were brutally murdered and the house destroyed by fire.

the basic principles Wright had laid down and develop their own expressions of them.

Wright had a feeling for the nature of materials and how to exploit them to their fullest in his designs; but he declined to explain how he managed to do this, and it is left to us to learn by examination rather than imitation. He was a unique individual who considered his best work to be his next project, always looking to the future. We look back on his life and work with awe and respect for his gigantic talent.

FRANCIS W. LITTLE HOUSE, (NORTHOME), WAYZATA, MINNESOTA, 1913 (OPPOSITE, ABOVE AND BELOW)
This has the largest residential interior of Wright's career at 55 x 35ft (17 x 11m). The house was threatened with demolition when a nearby Wright client, Don Lovness, contacted a friend in New York and arranged to have the Metropolitan Museum of Art purchase and dismantle it. Ten years later, after a wide search for candidates, they hired Thomas A. Heinz to design and supervise the installation in the newly constructed American Wing.

AMERICAN READI-CUT SYSTEM, PERSPECTIVE DRAWING OF TWO-STOREY UNIT, 1916 (ABOVE)
Although many believe that this was a system of prefabrication, it was actually one where the components were pre-cut. The various parts were noted on a plan and each piece was prepared and labelled, indicating its final position in the building. There were still many options open to a prospective owner and few buildings turned out to be exactly according to the plan.

These two-storey or two-flat buildings are to be found in
Milwaukee, and were known as the Arthur Richards Duplex Apartments. They were situated in a row and had opposite-handed plans which made up two sets of two buildings. They were the first to be constructed using Wright's American Ready-Cut System and all the buildings were stucco-surfaced.

Wright later incorporated the system into his other designs.

This perspective was prepared as part of the promotional material for the Richards Company of Milwaukee, Wright's client.

FREDERICK C. BOGK HOUSE, MILWAUKEE, WISCONSON, 1916 (LEFT)

This is a larger and more elaborate development of the 1907 Ladies' Home Journal Fireproof House for $5,000. There are several interior departures, probably the most dramatic of which is the change of levels between rooms, resulting in a welcome height addition to the living room. The roofed porches that can be seen on the Booth Ravine Bluffs houses are small, tile-floored sun traps on the south sides of the buildings, but the Bogk scheme has a small outside balcony above it, leading from a bedroom.

From the outside one might expect the living room to be dark because of the deep-set casement windows. This is not the case: in fact the living room is very bright, the thin, vertical slit windows providing extra illumination. Similar windows are featured in the magazine design and also in its first realization, the first Stephen Hunt house of 1907.

ARTHUR MUNKWITZ DUPLEXES, MILWAUKEE, WISCONSIN, 1916 (OVERLEAF)

These have now been demolished, removed in 1973 by the City of Milwaukee in order to widen the street. Munkwitz and members of his family seem to have been involved in real estate all over Milwaukee and this appears to be but one venture, certainly the one for which he will be remembered.

Arthur Munkwitz was apparently related to Frederick Bogk and both lived in the same neighbourhood.

ALINE BARNSDALL HOUSE (HOLLYHOCK HOUSE), LOS ANGELES, CALIFORNIA, 1920

At the time that the Barnsdall House was designed, it was felt that sunlight should be excluded from the interior as far as possible. This is why the very small windows are deeply recessed into the walls.

It does have an exotic, some would say Mayan or Incan look about it, but this does not appear to have been intended by Wright on any conscious level: it could be seen as an evocation rather than an imitation.

Wright prepared three different schemes for presentation to Aline Barnsdall, one a more typical hipped-roof design that included deep roof overhangs more like those of his earlier work in Oak Park and Buffalo. The final scheme, while appearing to have historicist connotations, is in fact a modern building with clean lines and plain surfaces. The formality of this elevation is not carried to the interior to the living room inside.

ALINE BARNSDALL HOUSE (HOLLYHOCK HOUSE), LOS ANGELES, CALIFORNIA, 1920

The continuous bands of detailing that trim the headline are to be found on all sides of the house, including the large courtyard which was occasionally used for theatrical events. They are said to be an abstraction of the hollyhock which was the favourite flower of the client and the plant that gave the house its name. The house was actually built in the middle of an olive grove, so it is all the more surprising that this fact was ignored when searching for a motif.

RIGHT: *A view of the living room.*

JOHN STORER HOUSE, LOS ANGELES, CALIFORNIA, 1923 (LEFT AND OVERLEAF)

Wright was to produce one of his most efficient houses for Dr. Storer. The plan, designed for a site with a significant pitch to it, had already been presented to a previous client, a Mr. Lowe of Eaglerock, who had decided not to continue. It is one of the best houses ever developed by Wright, the other being the Hunt house. Fortunately for Storer, the view across to Hollywood more than compensated for the deficiencies of the site.

Using a concrete block system improved from the one used on the Millard house, steel rods were added to improve the house's ability to withstand the earthquakes which are prevalent in California. The wooden, mullioned screen panel behind the perforated concrete blocks slides to the left on a set of upper and lower tracks and allows for ventilation to the bedroom behind; it is also a way of keeping the interior secure.

The Storer House utilizes several individual designs for the concrete blocks, but other block houses kept to a single decorative motif. However, the multi-designs seemed neither to detract nor enhance the overall quality of the house and may have been another of Wright's many experiments.

ALICE MILLARD HOUSE (LA MINIATURA), PASADENA, CALIFORNIA, 1923

The Millards had had a previous house designed for them by Wright in 1906, in Highland Park, Illinois.

The Chicago literary scene had once revolved around George Madison Millard and his wife, Alice, but the couple, specialists in fine books and antiques, decided to move to Pasadena, where unfortunately George died soon afterwards. Alice returned to Wright who developed a system of decorated moulded concrete blocks which would form the exterior of her new house.

These blocks are occasionally pierced, allowing light to enter, and there are operable casement windows on the interior to regulate air flow entering the house. The living room consists of a full two storeys and has a balcony overlooking it; the bedrooms look north towards the ravine which makes it such an interesting site.

A pool was constructed behind the house to reflect the building and the many weeping willows which grew on the site.

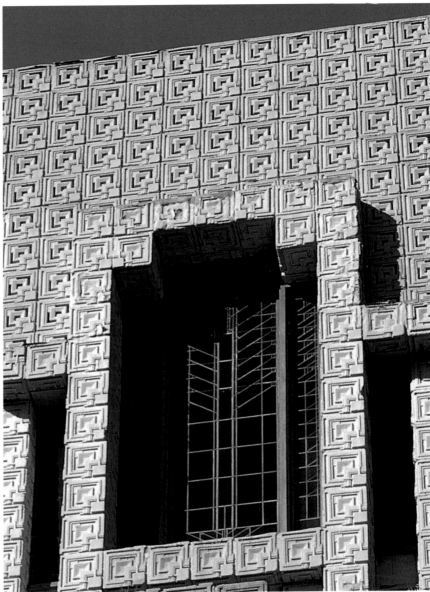

CHARLES ENNIS HOUSE, LOS ANGELES, CALIFORNIA, 1924

This is an imposing sight with a more European flavour than the Storer House, and has a linear rather than cruciform plan.

The largest single space is the central dining room with a living room alongside. On the far right is the master bedroom which is connected to the rest of the house via the living room by a columned hallway.

Situated between are a library, often referred to as Mrs. Ennis' room, the living room and the protruding dining room, all of which are large and tall. This is the largest of the California concrete block houses, built using over 20 different shapes and patterns of blocks.

63

EDGAR J. KAUFMANN, SR. HOUSE (FALLINGWATER), BEAR RUN, PENNSYLVANIA, 1936

This is probably the most famous house in America, inspired by Kaufmann, Jr.'s visit to the Taliesin Fellowship. It was meant to be a weekend retreat and was envisaged by the client as a sort of log cabin reminiscent of Wright's earlier Prairie houses. What he got, from an architect whose best work was considered to be over, was an exercise in modern aesthetics and technology which was an initial shock, but which he gradually learned to accept. However, as one of the earliest cantilevered structures which was built before the long-term durability of concrete was known, there have been some structural problems needing attention. The classic view of Fallingwater (left) makes it appear to be hanging high up on a crest or bluff, though in reality it is situated towards the bottom of the valley, as the view above shows. Nature continues to invade the valley and from the air the house seems to disappear into the rock outcroppings, so natural and appropriate is the setting.

PAUL HANNA HOUSE (THE HONEYCOMB HOUSE), PALO ALTO, CALIFORNIA, 1937 (LEFT, ABOVE AND BELOW)
During the 1930s, Wright had begun to experiment with geometrical forms – circles, triangles and hexagons – and how they could be applied to his architecture. The hexagonal or honeycomb grid on which the Hanna House is planned is not so evident in its façade. The only clue that there are no right angles are the

interdigitated brick joints at the corners. The walls follow this irregular line, zig-zagging back and forth. Understandably, the plan was not without its problems for the builders, who had had no previous experience in this area.

The restoration of the Hanna House had just been completed when these photographs were taken. It is now owned and maintained by Stanford University.

JACOBS I HOUSE, MADISON, WISCONSIN, 1937 (ABOVE)
The first Jacobs house presents a stark façade, the only windows on this elevation lying in the shadow cast by the eaves. As a typical Usonian house it was meant to be low-budget and much of the building work was done by the Jacobs family itself. It became a prototype for many more such buildings, some by other architects.

HERBERT F. JOHNSON HOUSE (WINGSPREAD), RACINE (WIND POINT), WISCONSIN, 1937

Herbert Johnson had recently weathered a complex construction project with the building of Wright's design for the administration building for his Johnson Wax company. It followed that Wright would also design a house for him, and the result was a modern development of the Willitts house with its pinwheel arrangement, that was set upon a large piece of land that also held Johnson's airstrip.

The house can be considered a one-storey building, although there are rooms below the master bedroom wing. There is a central pavilion which, in some parts, is two-storeyed and appears to be closed in from the outside and very open from the inside. The reason for the differing perceptions are the deep piers that frame the tall doors and windows of the four sides. From the inside, one can see out easily, while from the outside the appearance is dark and secluded as one is rarely looking in the same direction as the piers and they appear closed.

Pools and water always lend an element of peace and tranquillity to nearby buildings, making for pleasant contrasts of green lawn, red brick, turquoise pool and deep-blue sky. This welcoming corner of the house contains the library and entertainment area just inside the tall glass doors. Johnson's second wife did not care for the house, which eventually became a conference centre for the Johnson Foundation.

GEORGE D. STURGES HOUSE, LOS ANGELES, CALIFORNIA, 1939 (ABOVE)
Cantilevering the house out from the brick base seems like a natural solution to a very steep building site, and it is reminiscent of Fallingwater in its dramatic impact. The house has been admired for its design for over 60 years and yet the idea has rarely been used on the thousands of other houses built in the Los Angeles area. Essentially a single storey, it appears to rise through several levels from a solid brick base and demonstrates the amount of variation Wright was able to inject into a house that was essentially Usonian.

POPE-LEIGHY HOUSE, WOODLAWN, VIRGINIA, 1940 (OPPOSITE, ABOVE AND BELOW)
In its original location, the Pope House interfered with the extension of a new highway and was moved to the Woodlawn Plantation, near George Washington's Mount Vernon. Several years after this, it was discovered that it had been set upon an unstable layer of marine clay and would have to be moved a second time, to the extent of about 30ft (10m). This photograph shows the house in its third location and after it had been renovated.

Loren Pope was a newspaperman in Washington, D.C. *who had read about the Jacobs house in Madison which had cost $5,000 to build. Pope wrote to Wright and managed to get a similar house to what is now known as the Jacobs I house, but which was set on a sloping site rather than a flat one.*

The walls consist of a sandwich panel composed of a plywood core with solid cypress on both faces without common stud framing, a technique that would not be allowed by today's building codes. Pope wrote an article in House Beautiful, *praising his design, which was of benefit to Wright and brought him more clients.*

LLOYD LEWIS HOUSE, LIBERTYVILLE, ILLINOIS, 1940

Lloyd Lewis was a Chicago newspaperman who decided to abandon the city for what was then a country location in Libertyville.

As with the Sturges House, the main rooms were lifted off the ground for practical purposes to avoid flooding, the property being adjacent to the Des Plaines river which periodically burst its banks.

This was the first house where the extensions defined the garden, and concrete strips off the living-room piers made for mud-free access. This house has several levels, the living room being on the highest with the bedrooms on the lowest.

The interior is diffused with a warm glow due to the unfinished cypress used on the walls and ceilings, while light bulbs set behind the ceiling boards spotlight the fireplace, as well as giving general illumination to the entire living room.

**HERMAN T. MOSSBERG HOUSE, SOUTH
BEND, INDIANA, 1949** (RIGHT)
*The Mossberg house is less radical
in detail than most of Wright's later
brick houses, perhaps because it
was supervised by one of the most
conservative members of the
Taliesin Fellowship, Jack Howe, who
had been Wright's chief draftsman
for 35 years, and is more subdued
as a result. However, it is on a
larger, more generous scale than
most Usonian houses.*

ROBERT BERGER HOUSE, SAN ANSELMO, CALIFORNIA, 1950 (LEFT)
Berger had admired Wright for many years and had dreamed of owning a Wright house. After designing a Cape Cod saltbox for his family, to be located in the hills north of San Francisco, he realized how inappropriate the design was and contacted Wright asking for his help, explaining that he had little money but would undertake to build the house himself.

Few of Wright's houses are based on an equilateral triangle and fewer still use the desert masonry Wright invented for Taliesin West, though another was the unbuilt Charoudi House for Mahopac in New York. The house is in ideal condition, kept that way by Robert Berger's widow.

DAVID WRIGHT HOUSE, PHOENIX, ARIZONA, 1950 (OPPOSITE ABOVE)
David was the fifth child of Frank Lloyd Wright and his first wife, Catherine, and considered that at least one member of the family should make use of Wright's talents: what he got was a most unusual and striking design.

Placing a building on a concrete ramp is unusual given any conditions. In this case, the idea was to site the house so that it would catch every breeze as a method of keeping the owners cool in a hot and dry climate. There is no basement.

HENRY J. NEILS HOUSE, MINNEAPOLIS, MINNESOTA, 1950 (OPPOSITE BELOW)
Neils was a dealer specializing in building products which included granite, marble and architectural metals.

Wright was always willing to accommodate the wishes of his clients, whenever possible, and he utilized Neils' materials, constructing the house of granite with aluminium windows, one of the few instances of their use in the Usonian period. The house has a beautiful set of Wright-designed furniture that included a floor model of the pole lamp.

MRS. CLINTON WALKER HOUSE, CARMEL, CALIFORNIA, 1951 (ABOVE)
There may be no other Wright house with such a dramatic site, the house appearing to be at one with the ocean where it intrudes upon Carmel Bay. The house was almost new when it served as a backdrop for the 1959 movie, A Summer Place, *starring Sandra Dee and Troy Donahue. In the movie, however, there was a stairway leading down to a lower level which does not in fact exist. The house is still owned by the original San Francisco family that commissioned its construction.*

DON & VIRGINIA LOVNESS HOUSE, STILLWATER, MINNESOTA, MINNEAPOLIS, 1955 (ABOVE)
Although this is not a Usonian Automatic house, the clients, Don and Virginia Lovness, built the house with their own hands. Having had no formal or informal training in the art of building, but with a great enthusiasm for Wright's work, they learned as they went along.

While the construction was in progress, the family of four lived in a tiny trailer next to the building site: before leaving for his day job at 3M, Don would mix a large batch of mortar for the slightly-built Virginia to use when she laid up the stone walls.

When they asked Wright for this design, they also stipulated that they would want designs for several other houses or cottages to be sited around the small lake on their beautiful property just outside Minneapolis.

MAXIMILLIAN HOFFMAN HOUSE, RYE, NEW YORK, 1955 (RIGHT)
Hoffman was the man who brought the European sports car to America and imported Jaguars. He was a successful businessman and had this expansive house built for himself just north of New York City.

78

**THEODORE A. PAPPAS HOUSE, ST.
LOUIS, MISSOURI, 1955** (ABOVE)
*A red colouring was added to the
mix of the custom block used in the
construction of this house. It was
one of the first houses to overlook
an interstate highway, now
unfortunately commonplace.*